WHAT SHOULD NEW YORK'S NEXT MAYOR DO?

SPECIFIC EVILS TO AVOID
SPECIFIC CONDITIONS TO CORRECT
SPECIFIC STEPS TO TAKE
SPECIFIC OPPORTUNITIES TO REALIZE

BUREAU OF MUNICIPAL RESEARCH
261 Broadway
May 10, 1909

Price, 25 Cents

Resolved, That the Chamber of Commerce of the State of New York reaffirms the endorsement it gave in resolutions adopted last May, of the work of the Bureau of Municipal Research, and urges the members of the Chamber and all taxpayers of New York, to give to it their strong financial and moral support, to the end that, independent of any official or political agencies, it may be made permanently effective for the establishment of a businesslike, economical administration of the affairs of the City of New York

---

Offered to the Chamber of Commerce by its Committee on Finance and Currency, reporting upon the Financial Situation of the City of New York, February 4, 1909, and unanimously adopted

WHAT SHOULD

NEW YORK'S NEXT MAYOR DO?

Reflecting widespread discussion, the press of Greater New York has begun to center public interest in "New York's Next Mayor." Various minimum requirements have already been suggested: He must be an honest man, or a business man, or a lawyer, or a real estate man, a financier, a "stiff-back," or "at least six feet tall and handsome." The propounder of each of these seven requirements naturally criticises the limited point of view of the other six: the lawyer may not have organizing capacity or may dislike details; the business man may be unskilled in high finance; the financier may subordinate health, school, housing, traction or police problems to city debt, fire losses or speedways; a "stiff-back" may support a head impervious to new ideas; "six feet tall and handsome" may prefer dinner compliments to administrative responsibility

The more definite the community's expectations, the easier it will be to obtain, as candidates, men of "personality," reputation and organizing ability. Blurred public expectations mean a discredited next mayor. Specific things to be avoided, specific conditions to be corrected, specific forward steps to be taken, specific opportunities to be realized, suggest that New York's next mayor, if perchance an after-dinner speaker, should also be an after-breakfast worker. Whether learned or not, he should be capable of learning. If not a lawyer, he should be competent to enforce law. If not a banker, he should be competent to understand financial problems and to realize the supreme importance of city credit that will sell long term bonds at a premium and at as low a rate of interest as any American municipality. If not a business man, he should be capable of heading a business office and of applying business tests to himself, to his co-workers and to suggestions for expansion or retrenchment. However large his capacities, he should be big enough to see the limitation of his own eyes and hands, and able to select efficient subordinates to supplement and aid his executive capacity. If "six feet tall and handsome" he should be conscious that *he will be confronted for fourteen hundred and forty days not by a camera, an audience or an interviewer—not by one or two so-called "issues" inviting spectacular action*—but by innumerable definite questions requiring knowledge, decision and effective action as well as integrity

What the next mayor must do depends, therefore, on what acts the community itself wishes to perform or to prevent during the next four years, and what needs it wishes to meet. No matter what kind of man he may seem before election, the kind of mayor he makes will depend upon the results of innumerable acts that fall under the following heads:

Some of the Things New York's Next Mayor Must Do

1 Get squarely under and stay under the load of credit or discredit for work done, and for benefits or injuries received by the community during the four years of his leadership as executive, appointive and legislative officer. This brief does not attempt to distinguish results which the mayor can accomplish single-handed from those requiring coöperation of other elective officials. Even the present charter gives the mayor of Greater New York such a commanding position that failure to accomplish the right results is practically impossible whenever he uses effectively both his own powers and those of an informed public

2 Appoint 30 efficient or inefficient heads of departments to direct 55,000 employees and to spend about $90,000,000 yearly

3 Prescribe the standard of qualifications for 800 employees and officials to be named by department heads for exempt positions drawing $3,000,000 each year

4 Define the work to be done for positions which by means of their present indefiniteness permit responsibility to be evaded

5 *Promote discipline, or encourage laxness and demoralization* among 60,000 employees on a payroll of $80,000,000

6 Establish a definite point of view, sense of responsibility and interest in work of departmental employees or officials, which depend in large measure upon the character, reputation and business methods of the mayor's own office

7 *Make the mayor's office headquarters either for the city's business operations or for political, personal or social pull*

8 Conduct in a businesslike or unbusinesslike manner meetings of the board of estimate, for whose action he, as principal member, can not shift responsibility. He will determine in large measure the character and completeness of evidence upon which that board shall act in approving or rejecting propositions to use the city's taxes and the city's credit

9 Pigeonhole, "railroad," or secure open, fair treatment for measures referred by the board of estimate and apportionment to sub-committees selected by him

10 Protect, neglect or jeopardize the city's credit

11 *Determine whether investigations by the commissioners of accounts shall be thorough or superficial, partial or impartial, productive or wasteful; whether their reports shall be published or pigeonholed, and whether their findings shall be acted upon*

12 Exert an important influence upon scope, efficiency and cost of public education through his appointment of school commissioners, control over appropriations, power to investigate and power to veto or initiate legislation

13 Determine the character of consideration given by officials and the public to the annual budget that has now reached $156,500,000

14 *Determine the efficacy or futility of taxpayers' hearings on public matters,* the tone and result of which depends very largely upon what the mayor already knows and his ability and desire to bring out what taxpayers know. *If the burden of proof is placed on the taxpayer* instead of on the city official, *extravagance and misrepresentation are encouraged*

15 Determine the secrecy or the publicity with which each city department does the public business for which it is responsible

16 Determine whether the departmental heads currently act by guesswork and favoritism, or upon information

17 Affect the content, distribution and cost of city advertising, that last year totaled $1,000,000

18 Determine the consideration that will be given by the mayor's representative at Albany to bills particularly affecting New York City. *Many vicious or unwise bills will never reach the mayor for his veto or approval if all the facts available are adequately presented at Albany; fewer desirable bills will fail*

19 Veto or approve bills affecting New York City after passage by the legislature. The facts presented to justify veto or approval of such bills will largely determine later action by legislature and governor

20 *Determine in large measure,* by his selection of city magistrates and justices of special sessions and by inquiry into their methods and results, *the character of justice administered by criminal courts*

21 Determine the character of evidence necessary before his approval will be given to authorizations of corporate stock passed upon by the board of estimate and apportionment, which, during the last four years, have averaged $131,600,000 annually

22 *Determine, by demanding evidence* as to valuation, independent appraisals, alternative sites and city's need, *whether the city shall be mulcted or protected when purchasing real estate*

23 *Expedite or obstruct the reorganization of the city's business methods,* already so far advanced by the present administration that a passive attitude on the part of the next mayor will be impossible

Mayor's Program Should Be Constructive and Progressive as Well as Economical

Obviously, in meeting such alternatives, New York's next mayor must either inflict positive injury or confer positive benefit

Merely substituting the miser for the spendthrift will not appeal to public interest. *New York demands idealism, growth, achievable promise. It wants a broad-minded, progressive administration. Never before has it seen so clearly the defects of the past, the needs of the present, the opportunities of the future, or the methods by which defects can be corrected and desired ends obtained.* Therefore, the need for an efficient business organization to execute a wise and vigorous program. Both program and method concern four clear divisions:

Four Divisions of the Mayor's Program

(1) Immediate restoration of the city's credit

(2) Immediate correction of conditions that demand relief

(3) Related next steps which the community is prepared to demand and support

(4) Opportunities that will appeal to public imagination and conviction

In mentioning definite steps in each division of this program, the Bureau of Municipal Research does not pretend to make an exhaustive statement. Rather, it suggests action about which it believes there can be no controversy, the reason for which is based upon positive evidence gained by official and non-official investigation during the last three years

Immediate Restoration of the City's Credit

First of all the city's credit should be restored. Fortunately, success in this first step will release funds and energy for all the other steps

Impairment of financial credit has caused the city to pay higher rates of interest and to be hampered for funds in time of need

To restore city credit it is necessary:

1 To determine accurately and finally what the city owes. If the court of appeals should confirm Referee Tracy's decision that the limit upon the city's indebtedness does not refer to contract liabilities, legislation should be promptly obtained that will bring within the debt limit all that the city owes in excess of funds available for payment no matter whether bonds have been issued or not

2 Provision should be made for taking testimony relative to the eight questions not answered in the testimony before Referee Tracy on New York City's debt, which involve $50,000,000 of present indebtedness. *Pp. 81-82, New York City's Debt*

3 The mayor should undertake the formulation of comprehensive plans for future use of the city's financial credit and announce the determination that for four full years the city's borrowing power will never be used until after the presentation of all the facts for and against each proposal, so that urgent need may be distinguished from the undesirable, and from the desirable but unnecessary

4 The mischarging of current expenses to corporate stock when not specifically authorized by existing vicious laws, should be regarded as ground for the immediate removal of individuals responsible for such mischarges. It should be part of the mayor's program to ascertain where, if anywhere, in the city service, are bookkeepers and others in authority who do not know that aprons, kerosene, street brushes and bird seed are not properly chargeable against their children and grandchildren to appear as interest charges in future budgets. Where laws unwisely authorize such mischarges, they should be repealed

5 Issuing of revenue bonds against taxes proved to be uncollectible should be prevented

Impairment of the city's trading credit does even greater damage than impairment of its power to procure money when

needed at favorable rates. Trading credit has been impaired by lack of definiteness as to specifications of goods to be purchased; inequality of treatment of contractors and tradesmen; inadequate or inferior inspection of goods received, enabling one person to make deliveries which are inferior in quality and short in quantity, but insisting upon strict compliance with the terms of contracts by others; delays in the verification of claims before they are vouchered from the departments; delays in the audit of claims in the department of finance; delays in the signing and disbursing of warrants in payment for claims; preference to one class of traders and discouraging or making unprofitable the contracts entered into by another class, has forced the business of the city over to a basis of favoritism instead of competition

The results of these methods have been: to force the city to pay higher prices on wholesale lots than private individuals are required to pay at retail. The loss to the city on this account has been estimated at from two to five million dollars per year. Add to this the loss to the city due to the same causes on its contracts for construction, equipment and maintenance, and the annual tribute to bad management which has resulted in the wrecking of the city's trading credit may well be placed at from ten to twenty million dollars per annum. A large part of the added contract cost, to be sure, is not immediately felt, since it is shifted by being paid for out of fifty-year bonds, but each year thereafter must pay accumulated interest charges, and ultimately must pay the principal, due to the bad business of the past

Immediate Correction of Conditions that Demand Relief

1 Outline, publish and prosecute a plan for constructing and financing adequate transportation facilities

2 Rescind all existing authorizations for public improvements upon which work has not begun until a plan has been worked out by the city's engineers and department heads for schools, parks and playgrounds, public buildings and water-front developments; thereafter make no further authorizations except

for projects in conformance with far-reaching plans, based upon a thorough study of the city's needs for business, housing, recreation, etc.

3 *Adopt vigorous measures to eradicate preventable causes of tuberculosis, other communicable diseases and high infant mortality*

4 Strengthen the efficiency and fasten responsibility for all arms of the government that have to do with the protection of the poor against exploitation; inspection of foods, milk, tenements, dispensaries, weights and measures, employment agencies

5 Secure precedence for city prosecutions and if need be, a special court for city cases, and require efficient effort on the part of departments and officials that make and prosecute complaints

6 *Procure prompt and complete publicity of failure on the part of district attorney or the courts to vindicate ordinances and laws for the protection of property, health and life by prompt and efficient prosecution*

7 Ensure a thorough physical examination for the 25,000 children applying for work certificates, so that children may not begin their industrial life handicapped by incipient tuberculosis, bad teeth or other physical defects that can be easily corrected

8 Provide adequate administration and supervision of playgrounds, public baths, recreation fields and recreation centers and prevent these social services from becoming a new means of waste and exploitation

9 Secure better co-ordination of the city's hospital service, particularly its prevention and treatment of tuberculosis

10 Increase the quantity and efficiency of work done in civil and criminal courts by suggesting and demanding administrative reports that will disclose to the public work done, delays, reasons for delays, etc.

11 Make possible in the future the discussion of school policy from a basis of provable facts as to purposes for which money is spent and educational results obtained

12 Insist upon school reports and records which, because of completeness and adequate classification, will enlighten both educator and public and represent both the amount and the quality of work done, while at the same time disclosing obvious and urgent school needs

13 Stop giving private individuals exclusive use of park privileges. It should no longer be possible for newspapers to announce that "Mrs. H. and family are spending the summer in their camp at Pelham Bay Park," etc.

14 Stop continual destruction of pavement surfaces for corporation and plumber's cuts by providing pipe galleries

15 Make it impossible to create congested districts in outlying sections not yet built upon. Have the truth told about the deficiencies of the tenement-house law and secure amendments to correct it. Complete the abolition of dark rooms and school sinks. Stop renting city owned tenement houses to "middlemen "

16 Stop the erection of unsightly and illegal billboards on the principal thoroughfares

17 Remove all grounds for the claim that it is impossible, with the present police, to protect all districts of the city adequately; whether increased efficiency or increased number are needed can be ascertained by investigation

18 Investigate the non-enforcement of excise laws for the purpose of establishing the responsibility of courts, juries, district attorney, police and the law itself for such non-enforcement

19 In budget-making secure the co-operation of informed civic and charitable agencies in formulating the community's needs with respect to their special lines of interest

20 Publish a tentative budget as well as budget requests sufficiently in advance to permit of intelligent discussion at public hearings

21 Ascertain what it ought to cost to maintain roads and buildings, and vote enough (but not too much) each year to prevent depreciation

22 Stop the appointment of "corporation inspectors" by city departments at the corporations' expense, which frequently converts alleged protectors to taxpayers into blackmailers of private contractors and betrayers of the city's interest

23 Push the completion of the public library; municipal building; bridge loop; connecting link from Manhattan Bridge to transporation facilities in Brooklyn and Manhattan; police headquarters

24 Complete or permanently abandon the Bronx Court House, whose delays aggravate the losses the city will suffer from unwise location and unwise planning

25 Stop the issue of revenue bonds for purposes disapproved when the budget is made—a practice which deceives the public as to both the extravagance of officials and urgent needs neglected. Health work should be wholly provided for in the budget, so that health officials will no longer be compelled to claim that money for routine work in a tuberculosis sanitarium is essential to prevent an "epidemic" in the city

26 Stop the water waste by repairing defective, leaky mains and by metering, without extortion all consumers; bring the Catskill board of water supply under the control of the fiscal authorities of the city; subject all operations of the board to continuous public scrutiny; grant no more appropriations for this work in lump sums, but compel itemization in accordance with the purposes for which funds are expended; carefully review plans for construction and compel definiteness of plans before authorizing further expenditures; make impossible

controversies as to fact or policy among appointees of the mayor, which result in discomfort, uncleanliness and the spread of disease, because water, though wasted by millions of gallons a day, is inadequate for flushing streets

27 Include dock expenditures in the budget, so that the public may be kept informed of its return from valuable privileges leased, cost of recreation piers, ferries, etc.

28 Aggressively support by administrative acts and by instruction to department heads, the reorganization already begun by Comptroller Metz of accounting methods, operative records and reports, wherever the city does work, spends money or collects revenue

29 Demand monthly administrative reports from all departments similar to those now required by Mayor McClellan of the tenement house department. Employing an army of 60,000 representatives, the mayor cannot go to individual employees to see what they are doing; he can, however, exact descriptions of work done, that will enable him in his own office to know whether he is being discredited and handicapped by inefficient employees in any part of the city government

30 Stop the waste that is conceded by city officials, charter revision committee and joint legislative committee to be enough to make unnecessary for at least two years, perhaps for four, an increase in the total budget appropriations for current expenses

31 Extend and enforce the eight-hour day

32 Further the introduction of time sheets, that will not only establish presence on duty of city employees, but furnish a basis for deciding whether or not work done is commensurate with time spent and salary paid

33 Reduce city payrolls by securing from department heads, commissioners of accounts and the department of finance evidence as to the particular men who are incompetent or superfluous;

stop employing more bath attendants in February, when there are two or three hundred bathers a day, than are necessary in July, when there are from two thousand to five thousand bathers

34 Secure the establishment of a central purchasing agency, thus saving easily from two to four millions a year

35 Stop the purchase of supplies without competition; eliminate the middleman who has no office, carries no stock and has no capital except political acquaintance; stop paying several prices on the same day for the same supplies; stop payment in excess of market prices; stop paying for goods without knowing whether they are of quantity or quality contracted for; stop the ordering of supplies in excess of appropriation and postponing payment until new appropriation takes effect; stop charging supplies consumed last year to this year's appropriations

36 Establish a bureau of standards at once, without waiting for State legislation to secure a central purchasing agency. By making one brand or variety of supply serve the needs of a large number of schools, in so far as possible, the bureau of supplies of the board of education has effected very large savings. In one year on lead pencils alone $13,000 was saved by having the superintendents select a few standard kinds, any one of which would be good enough, and by purchasing from the lowest bidder the total supply needed

37 Stop waste on repairs through repair-shop records which show cost per shop. The chairman of the finance committee of the board of aldermen would not have been presented with services and property from the city carpenter shop, if such records had been on file

38 Bring about the creation of a court of condemnation of real estate, the correction of procedure for purchase of real estate by private sale, thus saving millions and excess condemnation

39 Discontinue abuses in connection with the leasing of city properties and privileges, and the conduct of the city's commercial enterprises, etc., by having made promptly an inventory of the city's revenue producing resources and by subsequent publicity as to the city's dealings with its debtors and patrons

40 Discontinue abuses in connection with city advertising that in the past have not only wasted money, but have subsidized individuals, organs of publicity and groups of men to foster further abuses in city advertising, as well as other public evils. Legitimate newspapers and journals will certainly unite in supporting a policy that treats city advertising as a purely business proposition, to be justified not by personal or political considerations but by provable results

41 *Increase the efficiency of the law department and demand greater publicity as to cases undertaken, cost, reasons for delay, etc.* Codify and publish opinions showing clearly where the haphazard practice of the past has resulted in conflicting opinions

42 Require the law department to draft city contracts so that the rights of contractor and city may be specifically and definitely fixed by the written contracts and not left to the uncontrolled discretion of department heads

43 *Stop the practice of securing from the corporation counsel opinions on a partial statement of facts to justify action or inaction on the part of department heads*

44 Provide for effective publicity of contracts, budgets, applications for special revenue bonds, etc., so as to prevent action by officials until after full knowledge of the facts

45 *Systematize the city's news service, so that it will be easier for the press to obtain authentic statements of the facts regarding important proposals*

46 Revise the conduct and editing of the *City Record,* which, though costing $360,000 last year, is now chiefly valuable as a source of profit to those who print it. Potentially a journal of great public value, it is now, for want of classification and able editing, a general depository for documents that are frequently wholly valueless

47 Give form, meaning and readability to department reports and compel their prompt publication

48 Facilitate public understanding of proposed charter revision by illustrations of defects and needs drawn from the experience of heads of departments

49 Maintain and extend the efficiency and independence of the two investigating and reporting bodies: the bureau of municipal investigation and statistics, and the commissioners of accounts. *If perverted to personal or partisan ends, or if compelled by lack of funds or inefficient subordinates to do superficial work both can do the city irreparable damage and contribute mightily to the demoralization of public service*

Some Next Steps Which the Public is Prepared to Demand and Support

1 Secure a gradual change in the date of payment of all or a part of taxes, so that by 1914 the city will no longer have to borrow money to pay its running expenses

2 Make a thorough investigation of the public school system, its curriculum, its administration, its plans for the future, its relation to private and parochial schools, its provision for children's health, and its principal needs

3 Work out and inaugurate a comprehensive plan for industrial training, with provision for studying and publishing the results of all plans tried

4 Take steps and outline plans for the ultimate control and use of the entire waterfront for public pleasure as well as public business

5 Establish, from departmental engineers and heads, a city planning commission to form a plan for city improvements, civic centers, schools, parks, public buildings, waterfront and transit development, with reference not only to the present requirements, but to those of the future as well. The season of budget-making should also be the season for making an annual program of necessary public improvements to be continued, inaugurated or completed during the succeeding fiscal period. By this means it will be possible to relate authorizations for improvements not only to an adopted city plan, but to the city's existing financial capacity

6 Provide for utilizing suggestions and answering questions from individual citizens as well as volunteer organizations. The recent reorganization of the bureau of licenses was precipitated by a complaint from a private citizen. It is not unlikely that more will be accomplished by a city administration which equips itself to deal directly with non-official agencies than by volunteer or paid commissions made up of citizens or of both officials and citizens. Officials should not be permitted to shift responsibility for failure to meet the city's needs to extra official bodies

7 Demand reports from charitable institutions receiving public funds, that will show clearly the amount of work done and that will prove compliance with a minimum requirement of efficiency

8 *Publish all reports of the commissioners of accounts*

9 Reorganize and reclassify the civil service, in order that titles may conform to the character of service and that salaries may be made to fit work performed. Much ground for criticism exists with respect to present civil service conditions, which cannot be eliminated without a careful study of the problem

as a whole. Tests should be provided whereby promotion and advancement may be based on efficiency of service and whereby the removal of employees on proof of inefficiency may be facilitated

Opportunities that Will Confront New York's Next Mayor

1 Ensure for Manhattan an adequate system of sewers

2 Establish a municipal museum and library on municipal subjects near City Hall, or provide for such in the new municipal building

3 Take steps, as soon as financial conditions permit, to secure for health and recreation purposes the ocean beach at Rockaway which has already been "added to the city map," and also to convert Blackwell's Island into a people's playground

4 Remodel the city's obsolete fire alarm system

5 Insist upon a thorough study of the "cost per unit" for efficient policing, street cleaning and fire service

6 Force down toward the disappearing point the annual harvest of 27,000 lives from preventable diseases

7 *Call at least one conference a year with responsible city officials of metropolitan New Jersey and of adjacent New York districts* which form part of the same industrial unit as Greater New York and which affect and are affected by New York's living and working conditions, assessments, tax, transit and other policies

To Ensure Efficient Service a Community Must Recognize the Merits as Well as the Demerits of Past Service

New York's next mayor should take as a starting point for putting his city's business on a business basis, improvements affected during the past three years in budget-making, in auditing of claims for and against the city, in accounting, in reporting revenues and expenses, and in facilities for audit and special investigation by the commissioners of accounts. In addition to giving unobstructed access to public records to citizen organizations seeking information, the present administration has already radically changed methods by which responsible officials may inform themselves currently about public business and through current reports make information henceforth available to the general public. Truly epoch-making (if completed) have been the steps taken during the last four years by the mayor and the comptroller, supported in numerous specific instances by their colleagues in the board of estimate and apportionment, more particularly the president of the board of aldermen. Especially notable has been the prosecution of these steps by the comptroller and staff of the department of finance. It is only by means of the ingenuous operation of these measures that any mayor can hope to do for New York City what ought to be done before 1914. To ignore the clear gains effected by the constructive work of the past three years would prove reactionary not progressive, obstructive not constructive

THE BUREAU OF MUNICIPAL RESEARCH

May 10, 1909

BUREAU OF MUNICIPAL RESEARCH

January 1st, 1906 Organized as "Bureau of City Betterment"
May 3rd, 1907 Incorporated as "Bureau of Municipal Research"

PURPOSES

To promote efficient and economical municipal government; to promote the adoption of scientific methods of accounting and of reporting the details of municipal business, with a view to facilitating the work of public officials; to secure constructive publicity in matters pertaining to municipal problems; to collect, to classify, to analyze, to correlate, to interpret and to publish facts as to the administration of municipal government. (Articles of Incorporation)

PRINCIPAL REPORTS, JANUARY, 1906 to MAY, 1909

1 Some Phases of the Work of the Department of Street Cleaning 30c.

3 *Salary Increases Not Provided for in Budget

5 *The City of New York, the Street Railroad Companies and a Million and a Half Dollars

6 *How Manhattan is Governed

7 Analysis of the Salary Expenditure of the Department of Health of the City of New York for the Year 1906

8 A Department of Municipal Audit and Examination 30c.

9 Making a Municipal Budget; Functional Accounts and Records for the Department of Health 60c.

10 *New York City's Department of Finance

11 The Park Question, Part I, Critical Study and Constructive Suggestions Pertaining to Administrative and Accounting Methods of the Department of Parks: Manhattan and Richmond $1.10

12 The Park Question, Part II, Critical Study and Constructive Suggestions Pertaining to Revenue and Deposits of the Department of Parks: Manhattan and Richmond 60c.

13 Memorandum of Matters Relating to New York City's Debt that Suggest the Necessity either for Judicial Ruling or for Legislation 30c.

14 *Bureau of Child Hygiene 40c.

15 Questions Answered by School Reports as They Are

16 New York City's Debt: Facts and Law Relating to the Constitutional Limitation of New York's Indebtedness 35c.

17 Collecting Water Revenues: Methods Employed by the Bureau of Water Register, Manhattan, with Suggestions for Reorganization 50c. **Digest of same, free on application**

18 What Should New York's Next Mayor Do? 25c.

REPORTS IN PROGRESS, MAY, 1909

Administration of Department of Water Supply, Gas and Electricity

Real Estate Transactions, Department of Finance

Tenement House Administration

Bureau of Supplies and Repairs, Department of Police

Series of Reports: New York as Revenue Producer, as Budget Maker, as Operator of Shops, etc.

---

* Out of print

www.ingramcontent.com/pod-product-compliance
Lightning Source LLC
LaVergne TN
LVHW011147110826
845150LV00008B/2567

* 9 7 8 1 4 1 8 1 9 2 5 0 1 *